DISABILITIES CAN'T STOP US!

STEPHEN HAWKING
Look to the Stars

Kristen Susienka

New York

Published in 2021 by The Rosen Publishing Group, Inc.
29 East 21st Street, New York, NY 10010

First Edition

Editor: Elizabeth Krajnik
Book Design: Reann Nye

Photo Credits: Series art (background) Ratana21/Shutterstock.com; cover Mike Marsland/WireImage/Getty Images; p. 5 Karwai Tang/Getty Images Entertainment/Getty Images; p. 7 Mirrorpix/Getty Images; p. 9 Bryan Bedder/Getty Images Entertainment/Getty Images; pp. 11, 21 Handout/Getty Images News/Getty Images; p. 13 MIGUEL RIOPA/AFP/Getty Images; p. 15 Danny Martindale/WireImage/Getty Images; p. 17 Bruno Vincent/Getty Images News/Getty Images; p. 19 DANIEL LEAL-OLIVAS/AFP/Getty Images; p. 23 https://commons.wikimedia.org/wiki/File:Physicist_Stephen_Hawking_in_Zero_Gravity_NASA.jpg; p. 25 David Davies/PA Images/Getty Images; p. 27 Christopher Furlong/Getty Images News/Getty Images; p. 29 Tristan Fewings/Getty Images Entertainment/Getty Images.

Cataloging-in-Publication Data

Names: Susienka, Kristen.
Title: Stephen Hawking: look to the stars / Kristen Susienka.
Description: New York : PowerKids Press, 2021. | Series: Disabilities can't stop us! | Includes glossary and index.
Identifiers: ISBN 9781725311220 (pbk.) | ISBN 9781725311244 (library bound) | ISBN 9781725311237 (6 pack)
Subjects: LCSH: Hawking, Stephen, 1942-2018–Juvenile literature. | Physicists–Great Britain–Biography–Juvenile literature. | Amyotrophic lateral sclerosis–Patients–Great Britain–Biography.
Classification: LCC QC16.H33 S87 2021 | DDC 530.092 B–dc23

Manufactured in the United States of America

CPSIA Compliance Information: Batch #CSPK20. For Further Information contact Rosen Publishing, New York, New York at 1-800-237-9932

CONTENTS

One of a Kind

Stephen Hawking was an English **physicist** and one of the smartest people of the late 20th and early 21st centuries. His ideas about space led to new ways of thinking. Many people know him for his work on **black holes**.

Stephen Hawking liked to talk about life and the universe, and he liked to have fun. He had a good sense of humor. But he also had a disability that eventually made him unable to speak on his own and required him to use a wheelchair. However, Hawking didn't let that stop him from doing incredible things. **Technology** helped him communicate with people all over the world.

By the time he died in 2018, Hawking was a well-known scientist, speaker, and author. His memory continues to inspire many people.

Stephen Hawking inspired many people around the world with his ideas about science and the universe. >

5

An Education

Stephen William Hawking was born January 8, 1942, in Oxford, England. He attended Saint Albans School when he was young and went on to attend University College, Oxford, where he studied physics.

Hawking graduated with a first-class honors degree in natural science in 1962—only three years after beginning his studies. He was very smart and had new ideas about the universe. While at University College, he met Jane Wilde. They got married in 1965.

In 1963, Hawking was **diagnosed** with amyotrophic lateral sclerosis (ALS). This disease slowly made Hawking's muscles stop working. However, his mind remained sharp. In 1963, Hawking began researching **cosmology** at Trinity College in Cambridge, England. He received his doctorate, the highest degree granted by a university, in physics in 1966.

UNSTOPPABLE!

As a teenager, Hawking liked riding horses and rowing boats. When he went off to university, he originally wanted to study mathematics. His father wanted him to study medicine.

Most people with ALS live about three to five years after they've been diagnosed. Hawking lived for 55 years after his diagnosis, which is much longer than many people with ALS.

Changing the Universe

At Cambridge, Hawking studied different scientific **theories**. One of those theories was the theory of general relativity, which Albert Einstein developed in the early 1900s. It talks about how gravity, space, and time affect each other.

Stephen Hawking used the theory of general relativity to study ideas about black holes. This research led him to challenge ideas about the universe. One idea was about how space and time begin and end in the universe. Hawking thought that space and time began with the **big bang** and would end in black holes.

Hawking became a popular professor of cosmology. In 1988, he published *A Brief History of Time*, his first book. He spent many years studying black holes. However, ALS slowed him down.

Albert Einstein's theories of relativity helped Hawking develop his own theories about black holes.

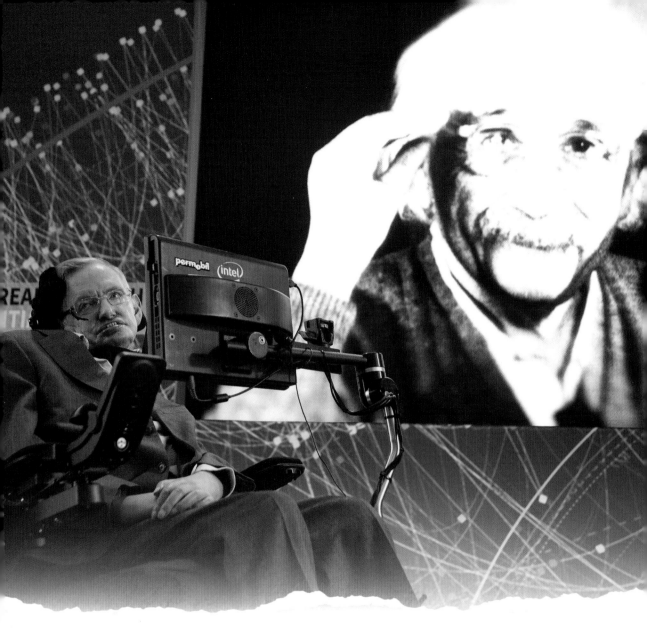

Albert Einstein

Albert Einstein was born March 14, 1879, in Ulm, Germany. As a young man, he was left alone in Munich, Germany, to finish his schooling. However, he ran away because he hated it so much. He was later admitted to the Swiss Federal Polytechnic School because of his high math scores. In time, his theory of general relativity changed the world. People realized how important his ideas were, and he won prizes and wrote many papers. In 1921, he won the Nobel Prize in Physics. He died in 1955 in the United States.

9

Hawking Radiation

Black holes exist throughout the universe. We're still learning about them, and we don't know a lot for sure. Many theories exist. Stephen Hawking suggested the theory of Hawking **radiation**. This theory states that black holes slowly let off radiation. The radiation slowly decreases the mass and energy of a black hole. Because of this, a black hole needs to add mass constantly. If it doesn't add mass, it will eventually disappear in a big burst of radiation. Hawking developed math **equations** that said this could be possible. Others began to agree with him.

People have detected black holes in the universe using special telescopes and math. However, it's unclear if Hawking radiation truly exists. Still, today many people think that it does.

UNSTOPPABLE!

Most people with ALS get the disease when they're between 40 and 70 years old. Over time, the person's nerve cells die and their muscles begin to waste away. This means the person can't move parts of his or her body. Some medicines help, but there isn't a cure yet.

This is an image of the first photographed black hole. The orange outline is hot gas that the black hole emits, or gives off. This black hole is in the galaxy Messier 87.

The Wonders of Technology

Stephen Hawking amazed doctors. When he was diagnosed with ALS, doctors didn't think he would live for more than two years. However, Hawking proved people wrong and lived with the disease for more than 50 years! Still, as years went on, his body became weaker. In 1985, he got sick and needed an operation. The operation took away his ability to speak.

Not long after the operation, Hawking received a special computer that helped him speak. It was difficult to use at first, but he learned more and became better at communicating in this way. Through the 1990s and 2000s, the technology improved even more. Hawking started using a special wheelchair in 2009. It had a computer on it that could read his eye movements and speak his words out loud.

Even though there were many advances in text-to-speech technology during Hawking's lifetime, he refused to stop using his familiar voice.

>

Hawking's Voice

Stephen Hawking was from England. Until his operation in 1985, he had an English accent. However, when he needed a computer to speak for him, his voice sounded different. An American man named Dennis Klatt, who worked to help people with disabilities, helped create the first computer Hawking used. The computer's voice sounded like Klatt's. Many people got used to Hawking's new voice. In fact, people had to get Hawking's permission to use the voice in movies or TV shows. The voice was called "Perfect Paul."

Strength from Family

Hawking had lots of help from his family and friends. He had three children with his first wife, Jane, who helped care for him for years. For many years, he refused help from anyone but her. However, in 1995, the couple divorced.

Hawking needed a lot of help to care for himself. Someone had to help him get dressed, take a shower, and brush his teeth and hair. Someone had to be with him all the time. It wasn't an easy life. Eventually, Hawking had nurses help him. One nurse, Elaine Mason, would become his second wife.

As Hawking's ALS progressed, his oldest child, Robert, helped Jane care for him. Hawking and his daughter, Lucy, were close, too. They wrote children's books together.

UNSTOPPABLE!

Stephen Hawking's disease affected him quickly at first and then slowed down. He began using a wheelchair in 1969. ALS inspired Hawking to do more with his life.

Lucy Hawking

Stephen Hawking

Hawking's daughter, Lucy, attended many events with him. Here, they're pictured attending the EE British Academy Film Awards at the Royal Opera House in London, England.

15

Overcoming Challenges

People with disabilities face a lot of challenges. Stephen Hawking had to overcome many tough times with ALS. One of the most important things he learned was how to talk using a computer. At first, he talked by pressing a button on a keyboard. Then, he learned to talk by moving a muscle in his cheek. A **sensor** on his glasses could tell when his cheek moved and sent the information to a computer, which then used a special system to create words. The computer was also able to figure out what Hawking might want to say.

Although Hawking communicated well enough to talk to people, write books, and give lectures, he continued to look for new technologies to help him communicate more easily. However, using these technologies often made him tired.

Without his special glasses, Hawking would have to type what he wanted to say with his fingers, which was very difficult or impossible. His glasses made it easier for him to communicate with people. >

Accepting a Challenge

Stephen Hawking didn't let his disability stop him from continuing to learn as much as he could and sharing his knowledge with the world. When he was diagnosed, he thought he only had a few years to live. Hawking said he once had a dream in which he was going to be killed. He took that as a sign to work hard in life. In the 1960s and 1970s, he studied hard, graduated from college, got his doctorate, and wrote and published scientific papers and books.

Becoming Famous

Hawking was a brilliant man. People in the scientific world thought his ideas were interesting. He spent a lot of time doing research and writing scholarly papers and books. He also wrote books meant for the general reader. His most famous work, *A Brief History of Time*, talked about gravity, black holes, the big bang, time, and how physicists have been working toward developing one universal theory to explain how time began.

Sometimes, though, Hawking's family felt like they didn't matter. Everyone wanted to meet and talk to Hawking, not his wife or children. Hawking liked the attention and even found it to be entertaining. Even later in life, Lucy Hawking struggled to get out of her father's shadow as an author in her own right.

UNSTOPPABLE!

A Brief History of Time is sometimes called "the most popular book never read." This is because, although Hawking tried not to use too many technical terms, many people struggled to read it because the subject was difficult to understand.

Much of Stephen Hawking's wealth came from the sale of *A Brief History of Time*. It's estimated he earned about £2 million ($2.4 million) from its sales during his life.

Traveling and Inspiring Others

Stephen Hawking often spoke about his ideas. Space, black holes, and the universe were the most popular topics of his talks. He traveled around the world and met famous people. Actors, **celebrities**, and politicians talked to him. He also gave talks online and to the public.

Some of his most famous talks were "The Beginning of Time" in 1996, "The Origin of the Universe" in 2005, and "Into a Black Hole" in 2008. He gave his last talk in 2018, shortly before he died.

Hawking also inspired many scientists who followed after him, including people such as Neil deGrasse Tyson and Brian Cox. They study the universe, like Hawking did, and looked up to him as a role model.

Hawking was a great lecturer. He gave a lecture to an audience at NASA in 2008.

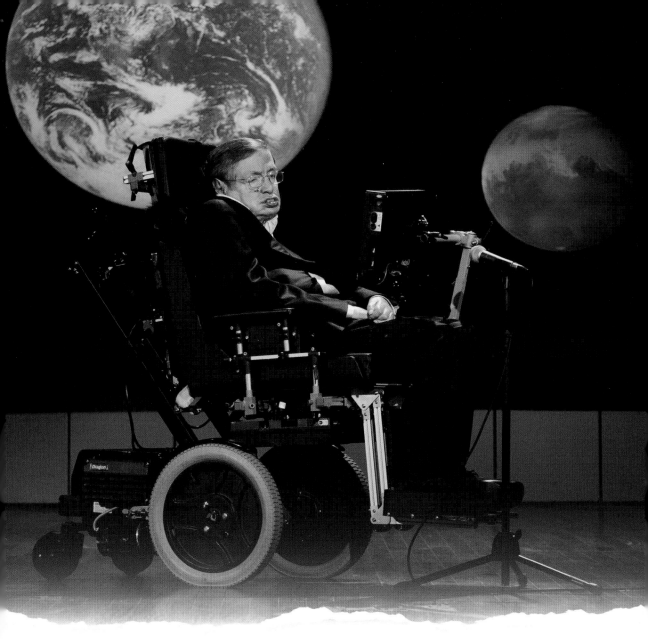

More than a Disability

Hawking received many awards for his work. Some of these awards include the Presidential Medal of Freedom, the Fundamental Physics award, and the Companion of Honor award. He was also a member of several scientific groups, including the Royal Society in the United Kingdom and the Pontifical Academy of Sciences in the United States. All of these accomplishments helped others recognize Hawking for more than his disability.

Acting and Having Fun

Stephen Hawking had a good sense of humor. He acted, usually as himself, on a number of TV shows, including *Star Trek: The Next Generation* and *The Big Bang Theory*. In 2016, he starred in a TV show called *Stephen Hawking's Favorite Places*. It took viewers on a journey to some of Hawking's favorite places in the universe.

Hawking's voice was also used in TV shows such as *Futurama* and *The Simpsons*. In 2014, the movie *The Theory of Everything* told the story of Hawking's life, how he handled ALS, and his marriage to Jane Wilde.

Hawking wrote and appeared in a number of documentaries, including one based on *A Brief History of Time*. The documentary focuses on Hawking's life and features clips of his lectures and interviews with family and friends.

UNSTOPPABLE!

Stephen Hawking liked to have fun in his wheelchair. He would dance in it. He also liked to drive fast. He once drove so fast he crashed and broke his hip.

Hawking wanted to travel in space one day. The closest he got was flying in a special airplane in 2007. It felt like he was in space.

Later Life

As Hawking got older, ALS affected him more. By the early 2000s, he couldn't move most of his muscles. Still, he kept learning, speaking, and thinking.

He also continued to write books. He wrote *A Briefer History of Time* in 2005 and *The Grand Design* in 2010. These books further explore the universe. *A Briefer History of Time* was meant to be an easier-to-read version of his first popular book, *A Brief History of Time*.

Technology also continued to improve. Hawking gave several lectures and interviews about the future of technology. He worried about the idea of **artificial intelligence**. He thought that machines could one day be smarter than humans. That could mean that machines could take over the world. He warned people about artificial intelligence, even though it helped him live.

Even though artificial intelligence helped Hawking talk and write, some kinds of AI may become dangerous if people aren't careful with them.

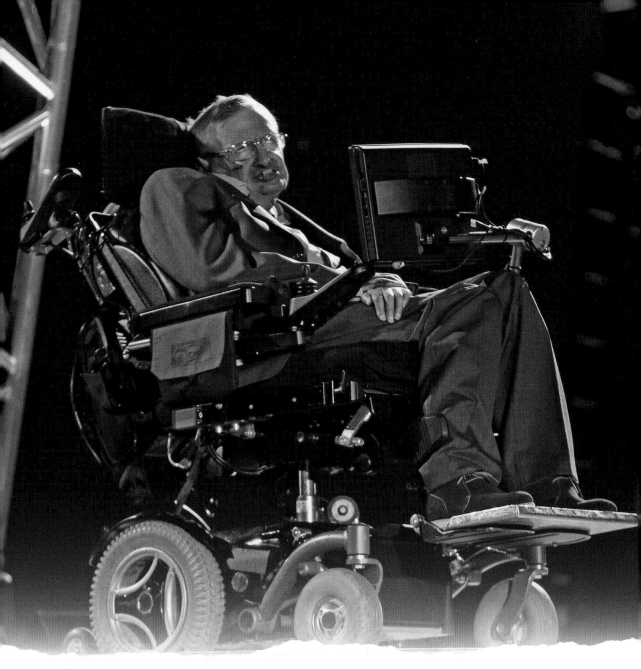

The ALS Association

Stephen Hawking worked to raise awareness of ALS. He was a member of ALS organizations in the United Kingdom. In the United States, the ALS Association informs people about the disease and helps people who have ALS. To find out more about the ALS Association, visit www.alsa.org. This website also has many facts and **statistics** about ALS.

Hawking's Death

Stephen Hawking died March 14, 2018, at 76 years old. His body finally gave up after battling ALS for more than 50 years. His funeral was held March 31, 2018, in Cambridge, England. His family, friends, and many celebrities attended, including Eddie Redmayne, the actor who portrayed Hawking in *The Theory of Everything*. On June 15, 2018, Hawking's ashes were placed next to the grave of Sir Isaac Newton, one of his role models.

After he died, people around the world wrote about Hawking's ideas and life. Many people bought *A Brief History of Time* and Hawking's other books. They wanted to learn more about him. Hawking is still remembered as one of the most intelligent people of all time.

Hundreds of people gathered outside the church where Hawking's funeral was held. His coffin was covered in white lilies, which represented the universe.

>

Living Life to the Fullest

Stephen Hawking always looked to the stars for inspiration and answers to his questions. Scientists continue to explore his ideas about the universe and black holes. His thoughts gave people hope that maybe one day, we'll learn much more about the universe. Maybe we'll even be able to examine a black hole up close.

Today, people still read Hawking's speeches, papers, and books. People also celebrate him by watching movies and TV shows about him.

Above all, Hawking lived every day to the fullest. He didn't let his disability stop him from doing what he wanted to do. He learned new ways of doing things. He used technology to speak. He knew how lucky he was to live at a time when this technology was available. It helped him live, and he was glad.

Stephen Hawking inspired others to study the universe and always reach for the stars. >

29

TIMELINE

1942
Stephen Hawking is born on January 8.

1963
Hawking learns that he has ALS.

1966
Hawking earns his doctorate.

1985
Hawking has an operation that removes his ability to speak on his own.

1988
A Brief History of Time is published and sells over 10 million copies.

1995
Hawking and Jane Wilde divorce. He marries Elaine Mason.

2005
Hawking publishes *A Briefer History of Time*.

2006
Hawking and Mason divorce.

2007
Hawking flies in a special plane that simulates zero gravity.

2009
Hawking receives the Presidential Medal of Freedom.

2010
Hawking publishes *The Grand Design*.

2018
Hawking dies at age 76.

GLOSSARY

artificial intelligence: The power of a machine to copy intelligent human behavior.

big bang: The idea that the universe started with a big explosion of energy.

black hole: An invisible area in outer space with gravity so strong that light can't get out of it.

celebrity: A famous person.

cosmology: The study of the universe.

diagnose: To recognize a disease by its signs and symptoms.

equation: A mathematical statement that two expressions are equal.

physicist: A scientist who studies matter, energy, force, motion, and the relationship among them.

radiation: Waves of energy.

sensor: A device that detects something and sends information to something else.

statistics: Information that can be related in numbers.

technology: A method that uses science to solve problems and the tools used to solve those problems.

theory: An idea or set of ideas that is intended to explain facts or events.

INDEX

WEBSITES

Due to the changing nature of Internet links, PowerKids Press has developed an online list of websites related to the subject of this book. This site is updated regularly. Please use this link to access the list: www.powerkidslinks.com/dcsu/hawking